THE NORWAY WAY

P9-CCM-933

to all those fortunate
soles who find themselves
in the magical north...
and to those who are
just trying to make
sense of it.

originaltittel: *the norway way*
copyright © originalutgave jenny k blake
copyright © norsk utgave Forlaget Vigmostad & Bjørke AS 2011

grafisk produksjon: John Grieg, Bergen
design: jenny k blake
papir: 120 g Amber Graphic

6. opplag 2017
ISBN: 978-82-516-5628-3

spørsmål om denne boken kan rettes til
forlaget Vigmostad & Bjørke AS
kanalveien 51
5068 Bergen
telefon 55 38 88 00
eller e-post til
post@vigmostadbjorke.no
www.vigmostadbjorke.no

Det må ikke kopieres fra denne boken
i strid med åndsverkloven eller avtaler
om kopiering som er inngått med Kopinor.

THE NORWAY WAY

the essential guide to norway & the norwegians

written & illustrated by jennykblake

Vigmostad Bjørke

This little book, despite
rampant generalizations,
is written with the greatest
respect for the norwegian
people, their culture and
the most beautiful land
in which they live,
the kingdom of norway.

Vær så god...

Norway is a strange, but beautiful place.

contrary to popular belief, it is NOT the capital of sweden, nor is it still inhabited by ferocious, sea faring vikings.

however, many norwegians do pertain certain characteristics of their adventurous forebears. they hold an affinity for the outdoors, the ocean, the mountains, fjords and forests. the norwegians are a hardy type and despite norway's wealth and prosperity they live their lives with a subdued restraint, they live in a way which respects the past but is mindful of the future.

← vikings didn't actually wear horned helmuts, although they were discovered in Denmark in the Bronze Age. the only similar example found in viking times were helmuts with birds heads attached, or in some cases, whole birds!

to gain an understanding of this unique norwegian way of life, the NORWAY WAY, it may be useful to firstly take a brief and non-concise look at norway itself...

norway

norway is a long, skinny country with a big, fat past.

NORGE

1814

10 000 years ago

the cold, thick ice begins to retreat and the first people appear.

AD 763

the fearsome norwegian vikings begin on their brave journeys...

800-1030

the age of viking rule

872

king harald fairhair rules large
parts of norway and declares
that he will not cut his hair
until the whole of norway
is united.

900ish

christianity arrives through
trading contacts.

1050

harald hardråde
founds oslo.

hmmm...
nice spot
to build
just here
i think.

1066

hardråde is defeated
in england, ending
the great age of
the vikings.

1130-1227

civil wars break out.

1397

trinity sunday. the
union of norway, sweden
and denmark is formalized
at a coronation in kalmar, sweden.

<u>1536</u> denmark rules norway

<u>1814</u> norway rules norway

<u>1814</u> sweden rules norway

<u>1905</u> norway rules norway

1905 norway steals danish prince
and make him king haakon VII

1923 the groundbreaking cheese
slicer was invented and the art
of pålegg changed forever

1940

the germans attack
and king haakon hides

1945

king haakon
returns from exile

1957
håkon dies, olav takes over.

1960's
exploration of the
north sea begins.

1969

oil was discovered & norway
was converted from a
country of "poor potato
and fish eating farmers"
to a country of "wealthy
potato and fish eating farmers"
virtually overnight.

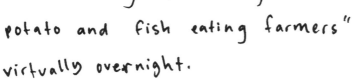

<u>1970s</u> the norwegians gradually moved to the cities with their newfound riches but they kept a love and respect for the countryside and they still ate potatoes and fish.

<u>1980s</u>

the norwegians gradually grew wealthier, but they were so scared of losing site of their wonderful lives as farmers that they imposed all kinds of rules upon themselves so they never lost site of their agrarian roots or the hardships they'd been through to retain their norway.

they reflected upon the countrie's tumultuous past. the numerous wars and invasions had left them a little bewildered...

this confusion lead the norwegians to celebrate all that is remarkable about their norway, their grand and majestic kingdom of norway.

they formed their own marvellous way of life - a love for nature, a respect for tradition, an ingrained sense of past. they formed a distinctive norwegian way of life, THE NORWAY WAY...

the norwegian male

(may, on occasions, be affectionately
referred to as a "weegie")

available in peace activist, environmentalist, friluftsliv,
handyman, familyman, entrepreneur and shaved headed,
glasses wearing, business suit models.

* friluftsliv model displayed

Cotton shirt: check, chambray or khaki only. (Stripes accepted at Majorstua)

scarf: not too tightly wrapped if you're looking at keeping your weegie long-term.

a really warm, woolly beanie: most weegies will be reluctant to remove these long enough for washing. hence the wet sheep smell occasionally detected.

windproof, watertight gore-tex jacket: either of the 2 leading norwegian brands acceptable.

Prickles: usually acquired on weekend cabin trips. treat with caution.

Y front boxers: no explanation.

loverly beige woollen thermal top.

gore-tex pants: khaki most popular. be aware if in the mountains in autumn you may well sit on a weegie before you see him.

birch handled knife: usually only used when cheese slicer is unavailable.

Woollen thermals: Y fronts also.

especially hairy legs: for extra thermal protection.

Sturdy hiking boots: leather, svede or gore-tex with a good spread of mud stuck in the soles.

woolly socks: moisture wicking for sweaty weegie feet.

accessory № 1
a sturdy backpack, sitting mat, turkopp & appropriate equipment for present season or laptop for weekdays.

accessory № 2
a trusty, bird-hunting, bell-wearing, stick-retrieving rover.

the norwegian female

also available in peace activist, environmentalist,
friluftsliv and entrepreneur, in addition to
kunstig, miss bogstadveien and husmor special.

∗friluftsliv model displayed

Clothing as per norwegian male, Y fronts included. Additional industrial strength chest protection also required for undulating norwegian terrain.

accessory № 1

a bundle of wool and gore-tex, and perhaps a norwegian child in there... somewhere.

accessory № 2

a contented, sturdy, durable infant willing to ride in strange baby backpacks, little carts behind bicycles and in some bizarre contraptions on snow.

accessory № 3

a life support system for accessories 1 & 2, containing various examples of norwegian cuisine as outlined in chapter 6. In addition, clothing and outdoor equipment appropriate for both in and outdoor use for temperatures between $-25°c$ & $+25°c$ recommended.

the n o r w e g i a n troll

: the essence of the generic norwegian
troll; earth, water, fire, air and a
good measure of dirty socks.

HABITAT: trolls can mostly be found high
up in the mountains, stuffed under
tree roots or awaiting your arrival
in dark caves or cheap, badly
positioned caravan parks.

light averting eyes: because all "nasties" try to avoid the sun; they're concerned it will damage their complexion.

hairy: so they can lay down flat and pretend they're a feild of grass to fool oncoming victims.

big nose: to smell out lost hikers, boaters or naive tourists who happen to wander into their realm.

walking stick: to navigate through the rugged terrain. Also used to keep occasionally explosive populations of lemmings at bay.

smelly: because as the common myth goes - if it looks bad, it probably smells bad to.

ugly feet: because ugly trolls have ugly feet

available in huldra, skogstroll (skautroll), dravgen, nixie, fossegrimen and jutultroll models among others, regardless, they're all pretty ugly excluding the huldra variety, who resembles a kind of cow woman thingy. * skogstroll model displayed

(under no circumstances to be confused with a nisse, a kind of nice little elfy thing)

the scandinavians as viewed by outsiders

danish   swedish   norwegian

the scandinavians as viewed by scandinavians

dansk   svensk   norsk

a fine day it was, the sun was shining,
when i took a walk through norway.

i searched, i searched, i hoped to find,
the key to the cultural doorway.

For the norwegians seem, just like their land,
the ruggedness keeping parts hidden.

Far away and hard to reach,
and entry seems forbidden.

everything will be okay.
everything will be okay if
i just do what the
others are doing...

norwegian mentality may
have been derived from the
days spent high, high up in
the mountains

the average
norwegian family...

lives in a lovely
little wooden house,

travels around
in a delightful
little stationwagon,

maybe to a small
cabin in the mountains
or by the sea,

has a playful little
dog that
enjoys fetching
sticks & dead things,

perhaps a kitty
that eagerly
watches small
birds through the
kitchen window

they may also have
a diverse selection of
cheese slicers in the kitchen,

and a diverse
selection of cheeses
to match.

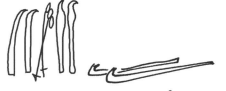

numerous sets of
skis for winter,

a couple of bikes
for summer,

numerous items
of woollen underwear,

and absolutely no
idea about what
a wonderful life
they have!

the wild norwegians
of the west coast
have the raging
waters of the
great norwegian
sea churning
inside them

the adventurous
norwegians of
the high-country
have the bold
and majestic
mountains towering
inside them

the hardy norwegians
of the north have
the hooves of the
grand reindeer herds
thundering inside them

the many norwegians
in the cities have
since lost their robust
inner spirits and now
they mostly just
have burgers.

a chain of self-conscious confusion:
five norwegians each wondering
what the other is thinking

the typical life cycle of a norwegian

a couple of wild, loving norwegians far out in the native forest

9 months later the arrival of yet another lovely little norwegian

who shall be cared for

and loved

and nurtured...

until one day that little norwegian shall itself return to its rightful homeland deep in the forest to begin the age-old process over again.

janteloven in practice

front elevation as seen from road

side elevation as seen from
behind the bushes

typical specimens of wild,
norwegian, nocturnal wildlife.

as the little weegies slowly grow
older they begin on the long
pilgrimage south to
experience all the
sinful delights of sun, sea
and cheap sangria.

social democracy

at   work

Norwegian Cultural Policy

* import as much opera, music, musicals, artworks, literature and artefacts from other places so that Norway becomes just like everywhere else.

equality

the great wonders of norwegian progress

№ 1

hydroelectricity

№ 2

telecommunications

№ 3

infrastructure

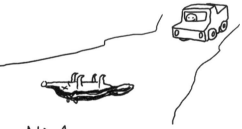

№ 4

døde grevlinger

after a brief discussion
all agreed that it was
unecessary to light the
fire in the lavvo today

borte er bra, men båt er best.

båt er bra, men hytte er best.

hytte er bra, men hjemme er best.

the confused state of a well-off norwegian

norske helse- og rehabiliteringssentre

upon the steps of oslo sentral,
cold and hard and grey.
lay the folk who had somehow,
managed to lose their way.
just like the leaves of autumn,
left wilting on the ground.
Security, faith and love,
either lost or never found.
people pass them by,
with a feeling of despise.
say a prayer and hope,
that they'll open their
blinkered eyes.

norway's top-secret
back-up defence strategy

the day the bamsemums collectors
got serious

THE POWER

the people

something very strange happens
to a norwegian as they pass through
the mystic magnetic forces and head aboard

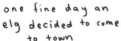

one fine day an
elg decided to come
to town

he wondered why so many
people decided to live in
such a crowded place
they must be very
friendly he thought

so he set off to
find some of those
friendly people and
see what wicked
delights the big
city offered

he visited a fancy
salon so he looked
just the part

he sipped a lovely
black tea at
theatercafeen

he tried lutefisk
at Gamle Rådhus
but he was
vegetarian
so he only ate
the mashed peas

he went shopping in
a big, shiny glass mall.
but nothing was made
to fit an elg

he went to watch
a movie, but the
cinema was not
made for an elg

he went sightseeing
but there were too
many of those friendly
people in the
way - so he watched
them instead.

this certainly was a
strange place he
thought. All these people
wanting to live together
but they didn't seem
too friendly towards
each other.

so he gave up trying to understand
the big city and ran back home,
relieved that all those strange
people did not want to join him
in his wonderful spacious forest

everyone called me a harry,
so a harry i was to be.
i bought a house in harryland,
it came with a harry key.
i found a harry wife & we had
a harry boy, we gave him

a fluffy dice as his very first
harry toy.
i drove a harry car,

with flames up either side,
its interior was purple velvet
& its wheels were extra wide

So now we live in harryland
as happy as can be,
my harry wife, my harry son
and little harry me.

the hardanger fiddle:
how to test for
a genuine norwegian

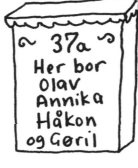

37a
Her bor
Olav
Annika
Håkon
og Gøril

37B
Her bor
Arvid,
Turid og
Sari

37c
Her bor
Eshkashem
muhammad
og aalat

phenomena norwegians secretly love

Jahn Teigen

electric candles

one night stands

the bottom of the fast food chain

Kaviar

princess madeleine

donald duck

harrytur

cucumber on bread

negerboller

kitsch christmas decorations

eurovision song contest

made in
norway

made in
norway

made in
norway

made in
italy

Various Royalty

england:
queen
elizabeth

africa:
nelson
mandela

america:
oprah
winfrey

china:
mao
zedong

denmark:
queen
margrethe

norway:
thorleif
haug

Storting.
stor ting.

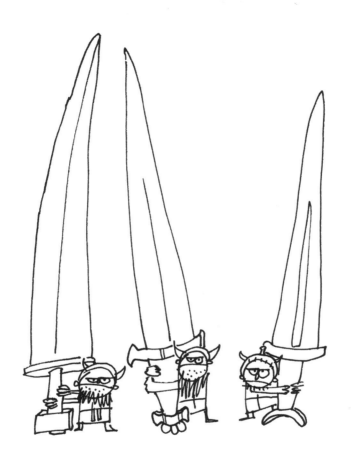

HAFRSFJORD AD 900

where why norway was united

business etiquette

paris

sydney

goa

moscow

munich

oslo

we're expecting
mr. hansen
from norway
today

they're leading
the market in
many areas of
new technology
and design

yes, the
norwegians
are miles ahead.
slick, sophisticated,
cutting edge

we're expecting him
any minute now...

"hall-ow dare."

where you find all the
ambitious trolls:
på vei opp trollstigen

a good little
norwegian
employee.

the rich folk of norway

bergen

Stavanger

oslo

egersund

a typical
norwegian
sunday
18:00

a typical
norwegian
monday
08:00

a day in the life of a troll

somewhere high up in the norwegian

mountains in a damp, dark cave.

i'll just be sitting here waiting for ya,

just sitting here waiting...

LONDON

OSLO

LONDON

OSLO

the official

"welcome to norway kit"

as required by all new norwegian
residents as a supplement to
the "velkommen til norge" orientation
programme as outlined on the back
of any kvikk lunsj wrapper.

Sitteunderlag
sitting mat. May double as a toboggan in dire circumstances.

Solbærtoddy
blackcurrant drink mix. good. very good. hot or cold.

Kaviar
fish mush in a toothpaste tube (no arguments weegies) it's just plain old fish mush in a toothpaste tube.

Ostehøvel
cheese slicer. it slices cheese, although since it was invented by a norwegian, thor bjørklund, many seem to think it has some strange, mystic powers & the world will fall apart in its absence.

Brunost
brown cheese. it's kind of sweet. it's kind of cheesy. it falls apart when the weather gets too hot, it comes in a multitude of varieties. it's pretty much representative of the norwegian people

Joika
canned reindeer.

Norsk flagg
the almighty norwegian flag. If you don't know what to do with it be sure to have a good 2 hours free and any norwegian will be happy to explain when, where & which one's appropriate for the occasion.

Knekkebrød
crispbread. because we all really do like that taste of cardboard.

Ibsen-bok
book by Ibsen. tales from a famous norwegian for those lonely norwegian winter nights.

Friluftslivsutstyr
outdoor equipment. no page is big enough to list all items. NB. all equipment must be current season.

Ryggsekk
backpack. QUADRUPLE stitched!

KAVINE

Ulltøfler
Wool slippers. totally acceptable in norway. you need not be over 70 or donned in a flowery nightgown with curlers in your blue rinsed hair.

Lommelykt
torch. great for the dark winters & may also act as a self-defence weapon should you be unfortunate enough to encounter a troll.

Ullundertøy
woolen underwear. essential.

Ullsokker
wild, woolly winter socks for wild woolly winters.

Engangsgrill
disposable grill. an essential summer accessory that's the death of many a norwegian garbage bin.

Kvikk Lunsj
much debate (presently unresolved) about if they're comparable to another unnamed chocolate bar (most foreigners won't notice the difference-if there is any).

beautiful forests, pure water, low population density...

norway is a wonderful place to live.

it's even rated us the most wonderful place to live.

it says so right here in the UN human development report.

you can imagine therefore, that it must be very difficult to get into norway,

because everyone must want to live there...

PASSKONTROLL

norsk!

very difficult...

the unseen hazards of the notorious norwegian
peat bog as demonstrated by a group
of unsuspecting german tourists.

the dark clouds cloaked the forbidding sky,
as i stepped onto the street.

oslo sentral i left behind as i
set out upon my feet.

on this grey day i hoped to find,
that little thing on my way.

that thing that was,
that thing that is,
the epitome of norway.

up the street i hauled myself,
past the beggers tins.

they no longer dance,
they no longer sing,
they just sit there by the bins.

I felt sad, i felt lost,
amid the neon signs.

none of which, i assumed to be,
of the quintessential nordic kinds.

renger
takk

upon the castle i finally came,
with a feeling of stoic pride.

So grand, so nice, so fine it was,
my elation i couldn't hide.

So there i stood, before its facade,
a little waving figure.

but the king wasn't home,
or he didn't see,
—perhaps if i was bigger.

So on my way i dolefully went,
with my head hung low.

if norway's heart wasn't in
the castle, then where was i to go?

i trudged uphill along a street,
of stiff mannequins and fake smiles.

pølser wrappers, plastic bottles and
paper cups, all heaped up in piles.

the further i went,
the slower i walked,
and my mind began to retreat

this quest, this search, this
soul-filled journey almost had me beat.

but then i found a huge iron gate,
with tall lamp posts on either side.

grand and mystic i knew they hid,
something special on the other side.

and there it was, that special treasure,
i'd been hunting all this day.

not in granite, stone or polished bronze,
but in the bushes it lay.

a little bird, a dusty brown, just
sat and didn't flee.

this elfin creature, and all
in nature, is what norway is to me.

a tourist returning from
an oslo shopping trip

recommended conversation topics:

and i thought he really liked me

the humble norwegian toothpick

assured

rude

tactless

thoughtful

discreet

creative

cool

prankster

expatriate

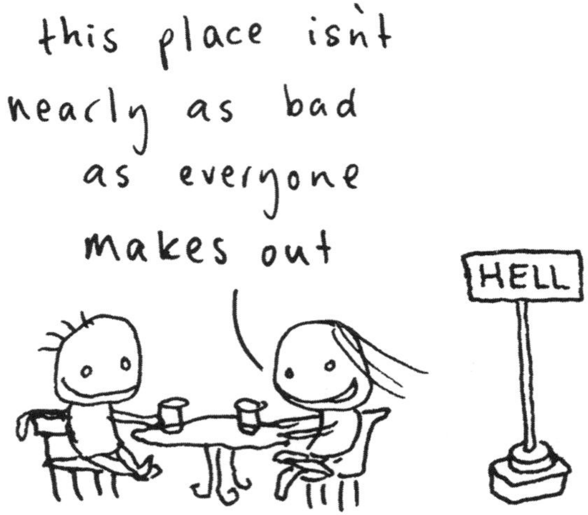
this place isn't nearly as bad as everyone makes out
HELL

a painted rose,
wool-covered toes,
an empty knitting loom.
i sat alone,
i sat upstairs,
wrapped in a sad green room.
the sky outside was
deep and grey,
its weight i felt bear down.
upon my heart,
upon my head,
upon this little town.
i sat in Runde
mid-winter it was,
with nature's guise all round.
i sat and listened
as the wind revealed,
her dark & wintery sound.

POLARSIRKELEN
- NAPAPIRRI
- CIRCLE POLAIRE
- POLARKRESIS
- A BLOODY LONG WAY NORTH

robert had thought of souveniring
one of norway's great landmarks
without first considering the consequences

i once took a train

and then a boat

and then i arrived at a most amazing

place somewhere in the north of norway

and it was amazing

trollveggen

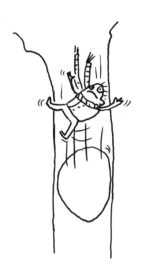

as a result of norway's escalating
obesity problems Kjeragbolten
will unfortunately no longer
be available for photo opportunities

here we are, way out in the rugged norwegian wilderness,

where some strange, mystic stone formations have been reported,

it's presently unknown by any historian the significance of these amazing structures. do they hold astrological relevance?

or perhaps religious?

experts worldwide remain baffled...

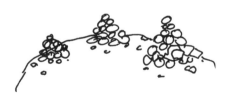

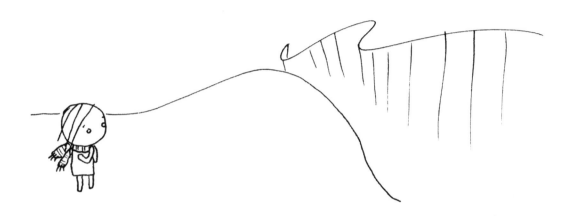

it was a cold, autumn evening. dark, clear, cold.
i took a walk up a still, empty road. the
secretive sky looked down upon me. the
infinite dark expanse looked down upon me.
me, alone on a cold, autumn evening,
alone on a still, but now less empty, road.
suddenly the sky began to sing. the sky
sang blue and green and iridescent turquoise.
it sang and danced and laughed at me there
alone on that road. then it sank. the sky
sank away and i stood alone in the darkness.
there was no applause. the sky just sank away
to darkness and i turned up that still, lonely road
and walked away from that laughing sky. that
dancing, singing, wonderful, but now empty sky.

abroad

norge

the closer you are to nature,
the more alive you feel.
the closer you are to nature,
the more dead you smell.

18°C BRAZIL   18°C FRANCE   18°C NORWAY

the less people you see on a
hike the more successful it is

hyttetur,
det er
moro det!

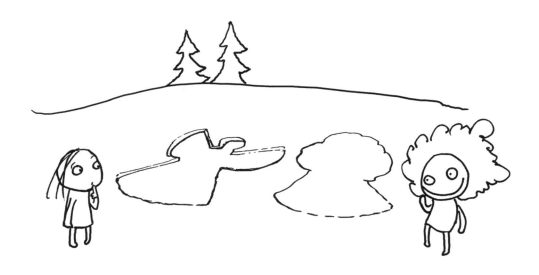

the art of making snow angels
was never quite the same after
"big hair" came into fashion

å få fred og ro

exposing nordic myth № 6: nudity

all the long, dark, cold winter

the Scandinavians must walk the streets hidden

wrapped in multiple layers, they quietly go about their everyday lives until —

the first flower of spring appears

then they manically (but understandably) tear off the layers

in a desperate search for the sunshine that has eluded them all winter

but the sun & light also brings tourists to these far off, mystic, nordic lands

and hence the visitors, some elated, some disgusted, travel back to their respective homelands to sit around in their mild winters wondering about those wild, free-living, naked scandinavians.

the norwegian
mountains make
me feel all alone.
without feeling
lonely...

a little norwegian lost
in sommer.

ut på tur - aldri sur

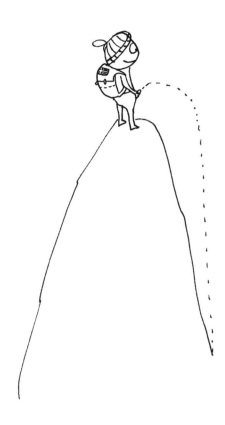

happiness

the beginnings of basejumping:
farmer hansen taking
his sheep to market

the fine art of "the walking
stick selection process" in practice

the wonderful smells of norway

freshly baked bread   ski wax   rain drenched dog
                            in december

snow on   mud in   summer
fir trees   the forest   thunderstorms

pølser på   freshly   the walls
engangs-grillen   mown grass   of old cabins

the good citizens all went
about preparing to escape
the hectic hustle and bustle
of the city streets...

for a relaxing saturday

afternoon in the forest

A hairy hat,
a slush drenched mat,
the tram wires
stark on grey.
An oslo street, 
i've missed the beat,
my scarf's begun to fray.
it's dark, it's cold, 
all life is dampened,
the nordic winter
stands here.
a silence,  
a restraint,
the light so faint,
i hope that spring is near.

den guddommelige pilgrimsreise

ordentlig norsk hyttetur

påske

the art of pålegg

recommended combinations

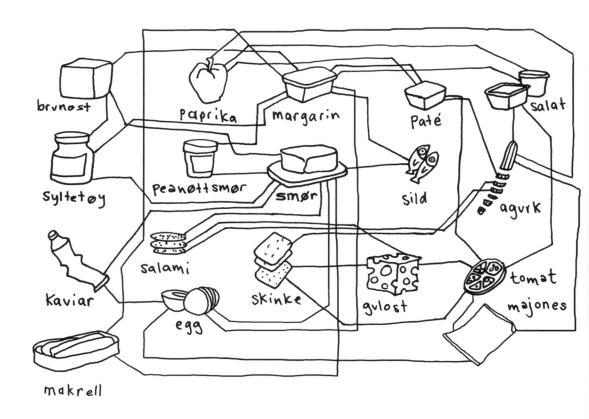

brunost

paprika   margarin   Paté   salat

Syltetøy

Peanøttsmør   smør   sild   agurk

Kaviar

salami   skinke   gulost   tomat

          egg   majones

makrell

NB. no responsibility held for misunderstandings
    of chart and consequently the creation of a
    potentially lethal pålegg combination.

① Construction

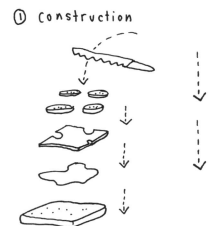

place your selected pålegg carefully onto your selected base. trial and error is, to date, the most reliable bases in which to choose the most appropriate base for your preferred pålegg combination.

DO NOT PLACE ANOTHER PIECE OF BREAD OVER YOUR BASE!

you have now created a typical norwegian "smørbrød". repeat the previous steps if especially hungry.

② Preservation

A.

mellomleggspapir

B.

C.

mellomleggspapir

D.

mellomleggspapir

take a sheet of custom made "mellomleggspapir" (lay between paper) and carefully stack each smørbrød alternatively with a sheet of paper to protect your pålegg. under no circumstances should a layer of bread be attempted. closed sandwiches are a rare phenomenon in norway and anyone seen eating them will be instantly treated with suspicion.

③ Protection

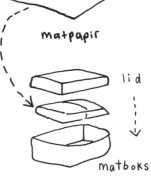

matpapir

lid

matboks

finally wrap your smørbrød stack in greaseproof paper or foil and carefully place it in a matboks, a small, aluminium box, to prevent your precious pålegg stack from being squashed.

close the lid firmly and be on your merry full matboks way.

119

Arvid thought he'd better call
into Knut's costume hire
before going to buy his
third bottle of wine for
the week

60kr worth:

czech republic

germany

norway

olav was in the lead when suddenly
the pleasant game of vinmonopol
went terribly wrong

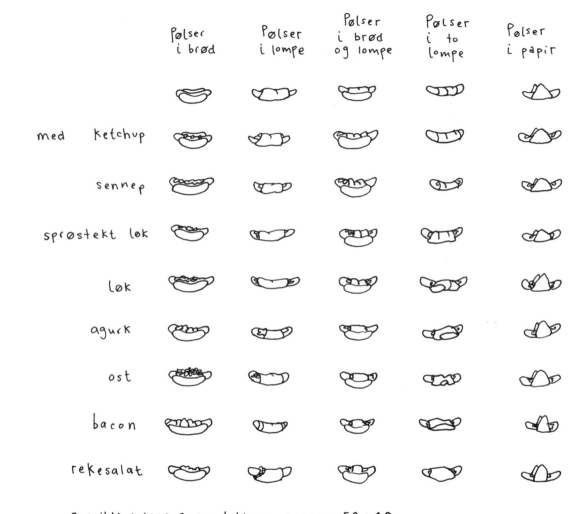

	Pølser i brød	Pølser i lompe	Pølser i brød og lompe	Pølser i to lompe	Pølser i papir
med ketchup					
sennep					
sprøstekt løk					
løk					
agurk					
ost					
bacon					
rekesalat					

Possible pølser permutations approx. 59049
—well in excess of the standard recognized illustrator's comfort zone, even without considering grill or wiener.

how to categorize a norwegian

CATEGORY A.

these norwegians are categorized by their tendancy to consume a pølse in a single direction from end-to-end.

personality traits

strong, focused individuals.
trustworthy, reliable, ambitions types.

Suggested occupation

debt collector, banker or train driver.

CATEGORY B.

working towards the middle of their pølser category B norwegians are often more flexible than category A norwegians.

personality traits

easygoing, tolerant openminded family types.

Suggested occupation

teacher, sales or fish scaler.

CATEGORY C.

wow... these creative and innovative norwegians will approach a pølse from any angle — often to avoid runaway ketchup.

personality traits

imaginative, carefree, happy-go-lucky, cheerful types.

Suggested occupation

often unemployable

ikke kødd med oss—
vi er på bærtur.

Modern day burning
at the stake

the meat kid syndrome

usually affects norwegian children within 12 hours of returning from a meat, beer and lolly extradition tour across the provocative swedish border. symptoms often develop under the heightened atmosphere amid too many trays of prime swedish rump steaks, danish chickens, beer in blue cans and multiple crumpled paper bugs half filled with fluorescent coloured, artificially flavored, sugar coated candy.

may experience outbreaks of psychotic laughter due to glucose overdose

Strained, averted eyes from veiwing multitude of colourful delights in oversized swedish shopping malls

Wobbly knees due to unfortunate combination of preservatives E340, E341, E471 with colouring E160a, E180a and E163b

large lolly bag clutched desperately in sweating, sugar-stained palms

symptoms are further agitated by the presence of three other glucose-saturated juveniles at various stages of hallucination, hyperactivity and hysteria in addition to the solitary adult in the volatile vehicle chanting "please don't stop us, please don't stop us..." as the four-wheeled, trance-consumed party makes its way over the seemingly endless bridge from the wicked delights of sweden to the scarey seriousness shrouded over the norwegian toll gates.

norwegians don't necessarily drink more
than other nationalities—it's just that
they drink it all at once.

rakfisk

tørrfisk

røkt laks

gravlaks

fiskepudding

fiske kake

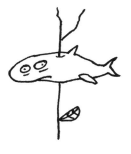

fiskepinner

fiskeboller

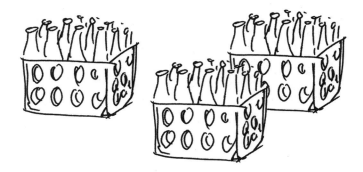

17th May

a norwegian on
his way to buy
beer in sweden

a swede on his
way to buy pilsner
in denmark

a dane on his
way to buy
ale in germany

a german on
his way to buy
wine in italy

an italian on
his way to buy
champagne
in france

a frenchman

pinnekjøtt

but one of the many
misfortunes of
Olav the unlucky

scene 1: a norwegian attic

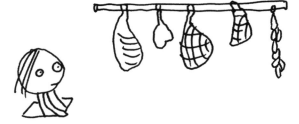

silence of the smoked lambs

and syver thought he'd found
the perfect hiding spot for the
last spoonful of tran.

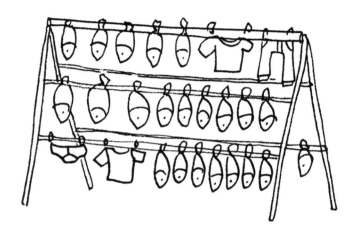

the great coffee cups of norway

skien

drammen

tveita

jotunheimen

colosseum

grönland

majorstua

bislett

frogner

nordmarka

finnmark

sommer

the great autumn debate

juli

januar

it was a little too late
when einar suddenly realized
the dugnad had not gone as planned

opportunism

despair

melancholy

desolation

anticipation

pure bliss

ikke dårlig klær
bare dårlig vær

Vår på landet

confusion at bodø
barnehage 15:00

the spring lonely hearts club

i've been waiting for the summer collection release for ages...

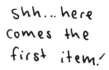
Shh...here comes the first item!

wow!

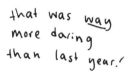
that was way more daring than last year!

153

DALE LUCIKOFTER FABRIKK

the official guide to unsatisfactory norwegian bunad

ketchup stain

sticky tape safety pin

with LV bag and Polo shirt

100% polyester

cross-dresser

with jogging shoes

pocket beer bulge

holey stockings

with football socks

incorrect sizing

combination bunad

Swedish national dress

nordmenn

nordmenn i bunad

the almighty knickerbocker salute :

to mark the annual norwegian
knickerbocker independence
day, that marvellous, liberating
day when someone took to a pair
of trousers with a pair of scissors.

GOD BLESS HALF BARE LEGS

a pregnant woman

a pregnant norwegian woman

spot the norwegian

there exists a common rumour amid
genealogists that many norwegians
have ancestral links with the pack-horse.

"how are we supposed to play CHICKEN with this silly fence in the way?"

it seems nothing escapes the
phenomenon   of inbreeding
on small coastal islands

the sandøya moped, motorbike & other wheeled apparatus family tree

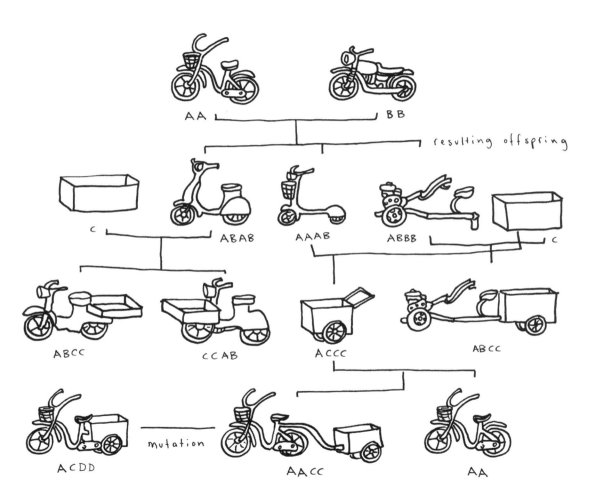

AA

BB

resulting offspring

C

ABAB

AAAB

ABBB

C

ABCC

CCAB

ACCC

ABCC

ACDD

mutation

AACC

AA

163

piggdekk for
underage car
enthusiasts

evolution

Korketrekker'n: the bob sled
run from the 1952 oslo olympics
open to the public, not
without consequences, both
fuller emergency rooms
and a sharp decrease
in hairgel sales.

a halling dancers dream

practice area

the <u>real</u> scenario of St. Lucia

new year's day –
the annual march of the
gingerbreadmen refugees

sankthansaften-pølser

they were nearing completion when the
pepperkakehus foreman almost lost it

pus was delighted someone had
accidently left a chair underneath
Arne's new advent calendar

so... what kind of life would you like next?

i'd like a norwegian life please. i'd like to live the norway way...

with walks in the forest,

and waffles on fridays,

and cabin trips to the mountains,

and dogs living under
the desks at work,

and cheese,
lots of cheese!

Sorry — but you don't seem
to have accumulated
enough points yet

but you <u>can</u> select
from a porcupine,
an african ostrich
or a miami jet-ski
rider...